THE WORLD ALMANAC® &  MENSA®

FIRST-CLASS
MIND
BENDERS

THE WORLD ALMANAC & MENSA

FIRST-CLASS MIND BENDERS

101 PUZZLES TO TAKE ON THE ROAD

DAVID MILLAR

WORLD ALMANAC BOOKS

World Almanac books may be purchased in bulk at special discounts for sales promotion, corporate gifts, fund-raising, or educational purposes. Special editions can also be created to specifications. For details, contact the Special Sales Department, 307 West 36th Street, 11th Floor, New York, NY 10018 or info@skyhorsepublishing.com.

Published by World Almanac Books, an imprint of Skyhorse Publishing, Inc., 307 West 36th Street, 11th Floor, New York, NY 10018.

The World Almanac® is a registered trademark of Skyhorse Publishing, Inc. All rights reserved.

www.skyhorsepublishing.com
Please follow our publisher Tony Lyons on Instagram @tonylyonsisuncertain

10 9 8 7 6 5 4 3 2 1

Puzzles and text by David Millar
Interior design by Chris Schultz
Cover design by Kai Texel

Library of Congress Cataloging-in-Publication Data is available on file.

ISBN: 978-1-5107-7606-7

Printed in the United States of America

Contents

Acknowledgments

This book is dedicated to Eli Shupe, Martin Owens, Matt Lee, Team Providence, teammate, and the MIT Puzzle Club, all of whom made my first trip to Boston/Cambridge for the MIT Mystery Hunt an unforgettable experience.

Thanks to my test-solvers:

- Ashley Goverman
- Martin Ender
- Natasha Jernigan
- Wessel Strijkstra

... and thank you for solving!

David Millar

Puzzles

Cube Logic 1

Which of the two templates can be folded to produce the exact same crate?

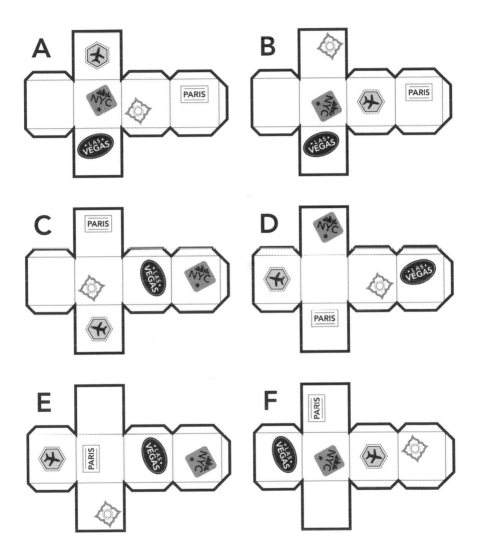

Rebus Travel Agency 1

This travel agency has some unusual ways of advertising travel destinations. Can you figure out where they want to send travelers?

ROCK

Transit Map 1

Use the clues to fill the bus route with letters to form words both northbound and southbound.

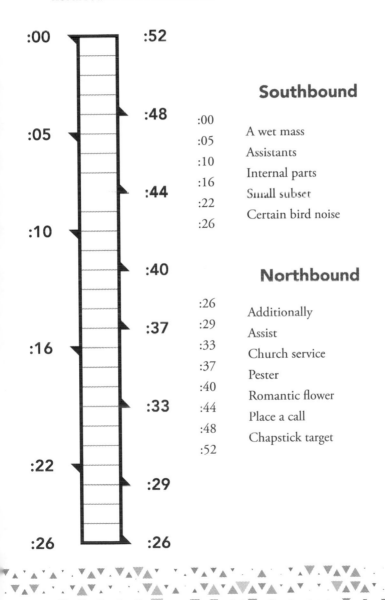

:00	:52
	:48
:05	
	:44
:10	
	:40
	:37
:16	
	:33
:22	
	:29
:26	:26

Southbound

:00	
:05	A wet mass
:10	Assistants
:16	Internal parts
:22	Small subset
:26	Certain bird noise

Northbound

:26	Additionally
:29	Assist
:33	Church service
:37	Pester
:40	Romantic flower
:44	Place a call
:48	Chapstick target
:52	

Scenic Route 1

Use the clues to determine pairs of words that fit the blanks provided.
Each pair will feature one shorter word with only some of the letters,
and one longer word that features all of the letters. When complete,
the numbered blanks will spell the name of a travel destination.

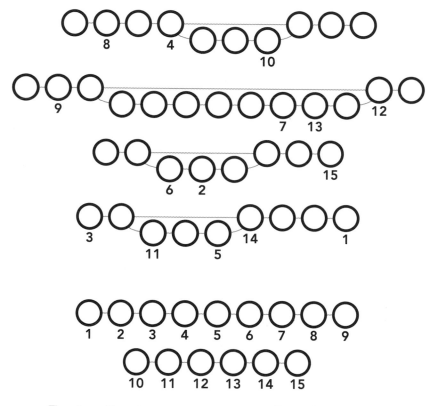

Faster Routes

Pairs well with "nickled"

Cousin's male parent

Coat's inner fabric

Place for a sister

Scenic Routes

Easy and quick

Endeavoring to hear

Painful and awkward

Relieved of a weapon

Rearrangement 1 and 2

Rearrange the letters in "GRANNY CAN DO" to make a tourist destination that has been enjoyed for generations.

Rearrange the letters in "JEERED YUPPY TREK PERK" to spell something that protein-loving hikers might take on the trail.

Symbol Sums 1

The sums of five combinations of symbols have been provided. What is the value of each individual symbol?

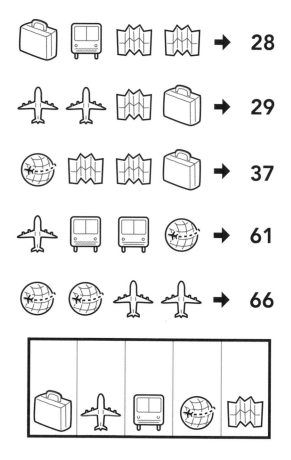

Word Sudoku 1

Place one of each letter from the word below into each row, column, and 2 × 3 box. A bracket between two squares points in the direction of the square with the letter that comes first in the alphabet.

ARIZONA

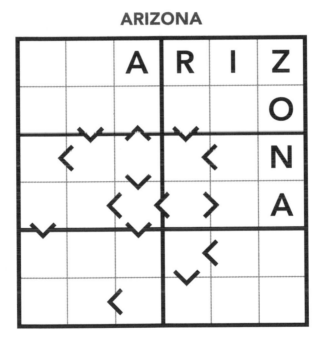

Country Road 1

Draw a single, continuous, non-intersecting loop moving through the grid and visiting each boldly outlined region exactly once. A region displaying a number indicates the number of cells visited in that region. Non-visited cells from two different regions mustn't share an edge.

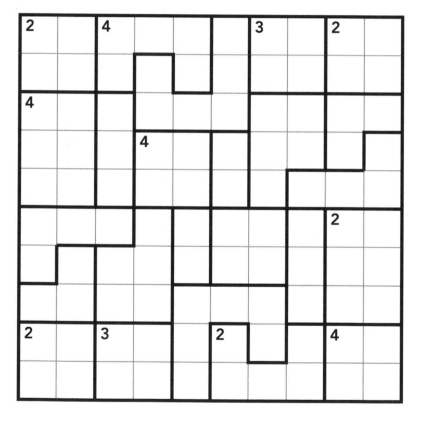

Lost Luggage 1

What a bummer! Each of the words below has lost the letters from the word LUGGAGE. Use the clues to determine which letters are missing and reunite them to complete the words.

V_ _ _ _ _   Offensive

_O_N_ _   Relaxation Place

C_ST_ _   Regal Residence

_ _ _ _IN_S   Tight-fitting pants

_ _ _ATIN   Gummy candy ingredient

Numcross 1

Use the provided clues to fill the grid with numbers. No entry may start with a 0.

A	B	C			D	E
F			G		H	
I			J	K		
		L				
M	N				O	P
Q			R	S		
T				U		

Across

A. Consecutive digits in ascending order

D. H across + I across

F. Digits that sum to 13

H. I across + Q across

I. T across − 1

J. Digits that sum to 19

L. D across × T across

M. F across in reverse

O. A perfect square

Q. Another perfect square

R. E down × I across

T. O across − Q across

U. I across × O across

Down

A. A palindrome

B. H across × 6

C. H across − 1

D. Consecutive digits in descending order

E. G down ÷ Q across

G. Contains every odd digit

K. D across + I across

L. D across − 4

M. T across squared

N. L down × T across

O. O across × T across

P. E down + L down

S. H across in reverse

Transit Map 2

Use the clues to fill the bus route with letters to form words both northbound and southbound.

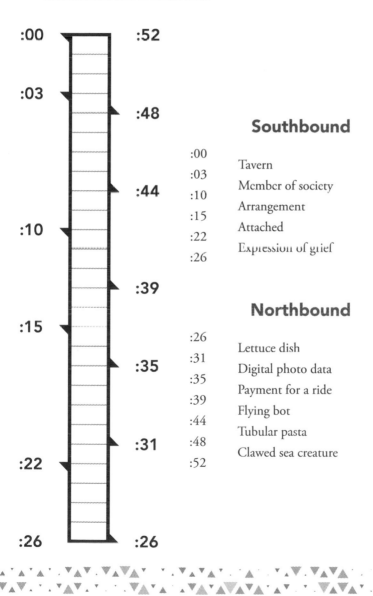

Southbound

:00	Tavern
:03	Member of society
:10	Arrangement
:15	Attached
:22	Expression of grief
:26	

Northbound

:26	Lettuce dish
:31	Digital photo data
:35	Payment for a ride
:39	Flying bot
:44	Tubular pasta
:48	Clawed sea creature
:52	

Rebus Travel Agency 2

This travel agency has some unusual ways of advertising travel destinations. Can you figure out where they want to send travelers?

Cube Logic 2

Which of the two templates can be folded to produce the exact same crate?

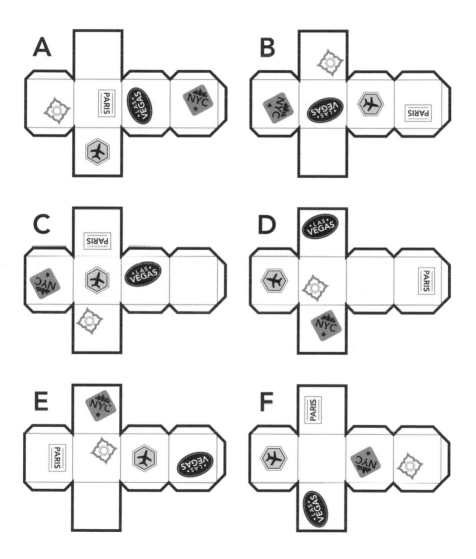

Throwing Shade 1

Shade some cells so the remaining letters in each row and column spell answers to the provided clues. Clues are sorted alphabetically by answer.

A	V	R	M	M	O	E	T	R
P	M	O	M	O	E	E	O	S
I	V	V	E	N	T	A	T	M
L	M	O	O	D	G	X	E
A	I	O	D	I	D	L	O	L
L	T	A	O	O	A	X	X	I
O	A	A	S	N	I	S	I	S
S	P	O	P	P	O	O	C	H
E	L	D	E	E	R	E	R	L

Rows

- Protective gear
- Person of age
- Totem or tchotchke
- Ski resort building
- Homer's bartender
- Place of refuge
- Man's best friend
- Paid ride
- Type of doctor

Columns

- Soothing succulent
- Sense of self
- Prescriptions
- Stew in sadness
- Stench
- Hot dog topping
- Place for travel
- Dangerous
- Mandatory

Rows Garden 1

Using the clues provided, enter a letter into each triangle to fill the garden. Each row contains one or two entries, and each hexagonal flower contains a six-letter word wrapped around the center. It's up to you to determine where to place the starting letter and the direction of the word.

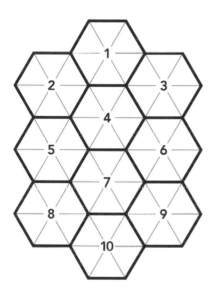

Techno and similar genres

Goofy cat term / Spanish father

Garlic paste / Rest

No-carb diet / Furnishings

Island nation / An energy source

A core taste / Elevated rock formation

Car type / Unit of land

Snag

Flowers

1. Plotted an area

2. Was shown through

3. Further in

4. Fashion workers

5. Fried chicken vessel

6. Gather livestock

7. Boozy brunch drink

8. Entertained

9. Fold

10. Yellow fruit

Scenic Route 2

Use the clues to determine pairs of words that fit the blanks provided. Each pair will feature one shorter word with only some of the letters, and one longer word that features all of the letters. When complete, the numbered blanks will spell the name of an iconic rail line.

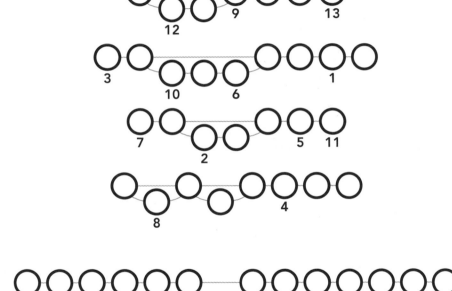

Faster Routes

An aquatic Olympian

Movie promo piece

Staying and waiting

Variety of game

Scenic Routes

Attack relentlessly

Bring the goods

City component

Plastic fabric

Numcross 2

Use the provided clues to fill the grid with numbers. No entry may start with a 0.

A	B	C	■	■	D	E
F			G	■	H	
I		■	J	K		
■		L			■	■
M	N			■	O	P
Q		■	R	S		
T		■	■	U		

Across

A. A Boeing craft
D. C down + 5
F. E down × 3
H. T across × 7
I. T across × 3
J. Digits that sum to 21
L. D down – 1
M. J across in reverse
O. A perfect cube
Q. Number of sevens in the solution to this puzzle
R. B down × T across
T. Q across converted from base 7 to base 10
U. P down – I across

Down

A. A across – 4
B. I across × 7
C. K down × 2
D. Jackpot!
E. P down + 7
G. (R across + 6) × 7
K. O across converted from base 10 to base 7
L. C down + 1
M. Popular convenience store chain
N. P down + I across
O. B down – 3
P. James Bond's alias in reverse
S. Q across converted from base 10 to base 7

Rebus Travel Agency 3

This travel agency has some unusual ways of advertising travel destinations. Can you figure out where they want to send travelers?

Transit Map 3

Use the clues to fill the bus route with letters to form words both northbound and southbound.

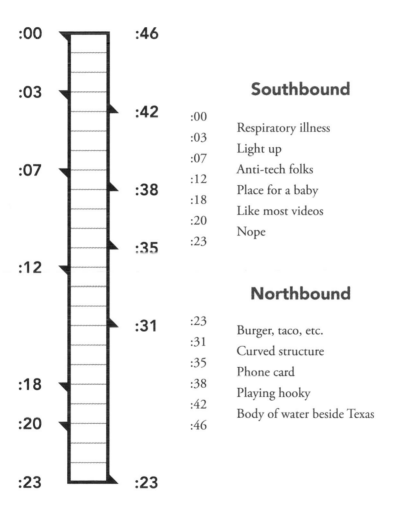

Southbound

:00	Respiratory illness
:03	Light up
:07	Anti-tech folks
:12	Place for a baby
:18	Like most videos
:20	Nope
:23	

Northbound

:23	Burger, taco, etc.
:31	Curved structure
:35	Phone card
:38	Playing hooky
:42	Body of water beside Texas
:46	

Cube Logic 3

Which of the two templates can be folded to produce the exact same crate?

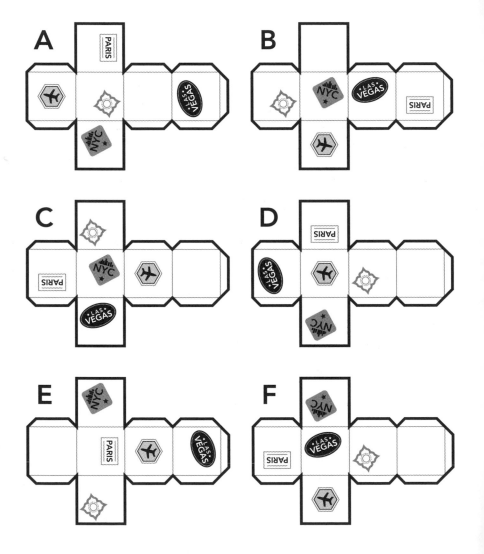

Symbol Sums 2

The sums of five combinations of symbols have been provided. What is the value of each individual symbol?

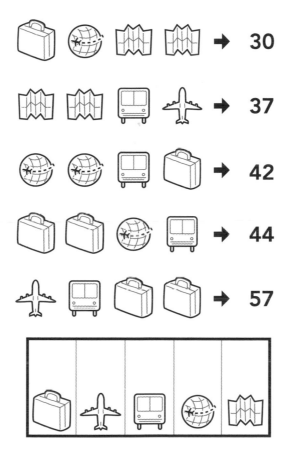

Rebus Travel Agency 4

This travel agency has some unusual ways of advertising travel destinations. Can you figure out where they want to send travelers?

Lost Luggage 2

What a bummer! Each of the words below has lost the letters from the word LUGGAGE. Use the clues to determine which letters are missing and reunite them to complete the words.

S_ _ _R   Common baking ingredient

DR_ _ON   Mythical beast

_ _ _T_N   Oft-maligned bread content

_N_ _ _   Heavenly guardian

_ _ _NT   Member of the FBI

Numcross 3

Use the provided clues to fill the grid with numbers. No entry may start with a 0.

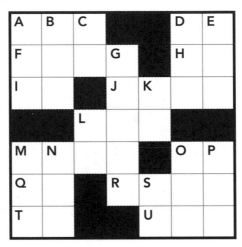

Across

A. A palindrome

D. T across – 1

F. Year Pan Am went out of business

H. I across + 1

I. O across × 7

J. Another palindrome

L. One-fourth of R across

M. F across – 10

O. Q across + 3

Q. F across – M across

R. Yet another palindrome

T. I across – 4

U. T across × 3

Down

A. One-half of L across

B. N down – 16

C. One-half of K down

D. Consecutive digits not in order

E. L across – O across

G. R across × 6

K. T across in reverse

L. D across in reverse

M. Digits that sum to Q across

N. D down + Q across

O. S down × 3

P. Consecutive digits in descending order

S. Playing cards in a standard deck

Throwing Shade 2

Shade some cells so the remaining letters in each row and column spell answers to the provided clues. Clues are sorted alphabetically by answer.

O	R	N	N	A	T	E	S	S
F	I	E	S	T	Z	Z	I	H
S	L	P	E	E	A	P	S	T
F	U	A	I	T	U	R	H	E
A	I	L	V	A	T	V	T	Y
E	N	A	T	C	T	E	R	R
L	S	L	E	O	I	C	E	P
E	P	C	R	I	C	E	D	E
R	E	E	C	C	O	R	D	D

Rows

- Go into
- Belief
- Celebration, briefly
- Soda necessity
- Kind of vine
- Intricate
- A verb tense
- Vinyl
- Shut-eye

Columns

- Home storage space
- Always
- Mountainous region in Asia
- Deal
- Clear with water
- Tear apart
- Location
- Tex-Mex staple
- Use a keyboard

Story Logic 1

Five friends took a birding trip to southern Texas and came back with five stunning photographs to share. Use the clues provided to figure out who took which photo and the order in which the photos were taken.

	First	Second	Third	Fourth	Fifth	American redstart	Black skimmer	Cerulean warbler	Roseate spoonbill	Scarlet tanager
Alan										
Colby										
Eli										
Evan										
Mark										
American redstart										
Black skimmer										
Cerulean warbler										
Roseate spoonbill										
Scarlet tanager										

1. Eli's prize photo was taken after someone photographed the roseate spoonbill.

2. The black skimmer was not photographed first or last.

3. Alan photographed either the American redstart or scarlet tanager — whichever was photographed later between the two.

4. The American redstart was photographed next after Evan's photograph.

5. The cerulean warbler, which was photographed by Colby or Mark, was not the first bird photographed.

6. The roseate spoonbill was photographed before Colby took his photograph.

7. The black skimmer was photographed between the American redstart and Alan's photograph in some order.

8. Eli did not photograph the American redstart.

9. Mark did not take the second photograph.

Rearrangement 3 and 4

Rearrange the letters in "FIANCE TROLLEY" to spell a town where a handsome fella might take a tram ride to the Cathedral of Santa Maria del Fiore.

Rearrange the letters in "LITTLE HUMAN REST" to spell a way to get around the airport with a bit less walking.

Rows Garden 2

Using the clues provided, enter a letter into each triangle to fill the garden. Each row contains one or two entries, and each hexagonal flower contains a six-letter word wrapped around the center. It's up to you to determine where to place the starting letter and the direction of the word.

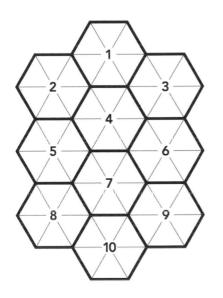

Metal box

Three full turns

Stench / Cookie, cupcake topping

Path or itinerary / Traitor

Post event fallout

Unskilled to a fault / Inactive

Novel appearance / Satellite

Type of lodge

Flowers

1. Set up blaze

2. Acted upon

3. Doodad

4. System used abroad

5. Groovy, man!

6. Despise

7. Allow

8. Theater

9. Pho component

10. Exonym for Inuit and Yupik peoples

Country Road 2

Draw a single, continuous, non-intersecting loop moving through the grid and visiting each boldly outlined region exactly once. A region displaying a number indicates the number of cells visited in that region. Non-visited cells from two different regions mustn't share an edge.

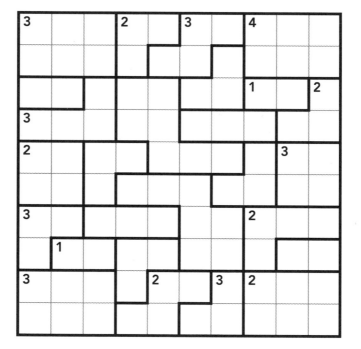

Throwing Shade 3

Shade some cells so the remaining letters in each row and column spell answers to the provided clues. Clues are sorted alphabetically by answer.

H	B	O	L	S	D	S	L	Y
F	E	A	E	O	E	T	D	D
L	A	O	W	B	Y	E	E	R
O	C	A	R	E	S	T	O	E
U	H	A	O	L	Y	U	L	Y
O	C	R	E	E	E	O	K	S
W	O	U	O	U	R	N	D	E
E	D	O	D	G	T	M	E	R
R	Y	R	Y	R	D	E	R	T

Rows

- One in charge
- Common house pet
- Boundary
- Stream
- Boughs used in holiday decor
- A representative
- Name-brand cookie
- Moving truck brand
- Wrapped

Columns

- Sandy location
- Alcohol-free
- One with seniority
- Glanced
- Plant part
- Item on a boat
- Deck
- Rock
- Buzz's pal

Numcross 4

Use the provided clues to fill the grid with numbers. No entry may start with a 0.

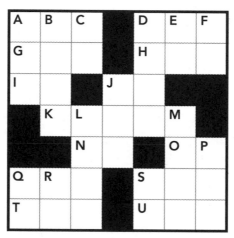

Across

A. J across × F down

D. J across × 12

G. E down × 8

H. O across + 18

I. One-third of J down

J. Sum of the digits in C down

K. M down × 5

N. One-fifth of O across

O. One-sixth of P down

Q. T across − R down

S. Digits that sum to J across

T. Q down × 10

U. S across + F down

Down

A. R down × 9

B. Consecutive digits in descending order

C. E down + 7

D. A palindrome

E. F down + 8

F. N across + 4

J. Contains one of each unique odd digit in K across

L. A multiple of R down

M. One-fifth of K across

P. O across × 6

Q. J across × 5

R. A perfect square

S. J across × 4

Rebus Travel Agency 5

This travel agency has some unusual ways of advertising travel destinations. Can you figure out where they want to send travelers?

Story Logic 2

The hustle and bustle of being a travel agent never ends! Use the clues to match up the clients with their planned vacation times and preferred destinations.

	Early June	Late June	Early July	Late July	Early August	Hawaii	Las Vegas	Los Angeles	NYC	Seattle
Carly										
Dawn										
Dinesh										
Marco										
Miguel										
Hawaii										
Las Vegas										
Los Angeles										
NYC										
Seattle										

1. The two destinations starting with L were booked for the two clients with names starting with D.

2. The trip to New York City was scheduled to occur before Marco's trip.

3. The Seattle trip, which is not scheduled in June, was for either Carly or Miguel.

4. Dinesh is not taking his trip in July.

5. The Las Vegas trip was either the first or last of this batch of trips.

6. Dinesh plans to travel the same month someone goes to Los Angeles.

7. The next trip after Dawn's trip is the one to New York City.

8. The late July trip is not to Hawaii.

9. Dawn and Carly both planned trips to the same coast.

Cube Logic 4

Which of the four foldable patterns can be folded to make the crate displayed?

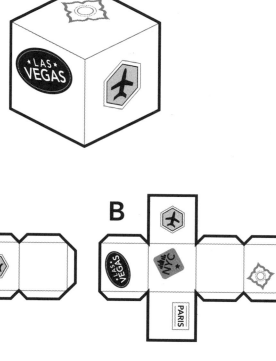

A

B

C

D

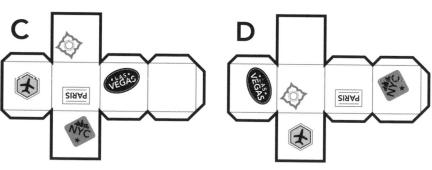

Word Sudoku 2

Place one of each letter from the word below into each row, column, and 2 × 3 box. (Ignore repeated letters.) A bracket between two squares points in the direction of the square with the letter that comes first in the alphabet.

MISSOURI

Transit Map 4

Use the clues to fill the bus route with letters to form words both northbound and southbound.

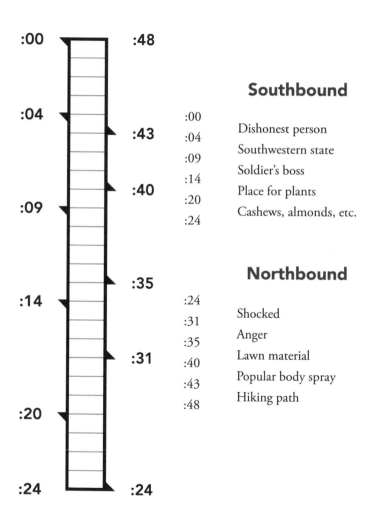

Southbound

:00
:04   Dishonest person
:09   Southwestern state
:14   Soldier's boss
:20   Place for plants
:24   Cashews, almonds, etc.

Northbound

:24
:31   Shocked
:35   Anger
:40   Lawn material
:43   Popular body spray
:48   Hiking path

Rows Garden 3

Using the clues provided, enter a letter into each triangle to fill the garden. Each row contains one or two entries, and each hexagonal flower contains a six-letter word wrapped around the center. It's up to you to determine where to place the starting letter and the direction of the word.

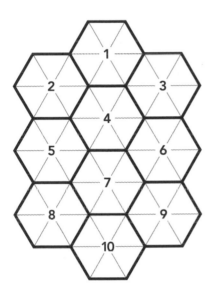

Actor Hanks

Kitchen gadget / Red Muppet

Flying ice ball / Body art, for short

Politician, usually / Charming gal

School punishment

Make spiral or twist / Hot and dry

Earthen dam / Combine fully

Message to lost loved one?

Flowers

1. Away from others
2. Lock in
3. Not quite
4. Improved
5. Clean meticulously

6. Toy train brand
7. Temporary home
8. Pivot
9. Tricky question
10. Realm

Rearrangement 5 and 6

Rearrange the letters in "FEATURING LIMO" to make an activity at many tourist spots where you might bounce a ball off of a vehicle.

Rearrange the letters in "BACKTRACK PIPING" to spell a thrifty excursion that a plumber might save up to take.

Throwing Shade 4

Shade some cells so the remaining letters in each row and column spell answers to the provided clues. Clues are sorted alphabetically by answer.

S	O	B	D	B	E	R	E	R
T	P	E	U	R	G	A	P	S
R	R	E	S	O	D	I	R	T
R	O	A	N	T	G	G	A	E
E	D	C	I	T	D	V	I	T
E	T	O	D	E	G	E	G	E
T	E	C	R	H	A	R	P	S
R	R	N	E	S	S	T	T	E
S	H	H	O	W	P	S	O	P

Rows

- Outermost part
- Change
- Fury
- Leisure destination
- Take it easy
- Place of business
- Serious
- Skilled worker
- Snares, for example

Columns

- Sandy spot
- Breakfast protein
- Command
- Expert
- Sewer rodent
- Type of IRA
- Entree's partner
- Make tea
- Lines on a map

Numcross 5

Use the provided clues to fill the grid with numbers. No entry may start with a 0.

A	B	C		D	E	F
G				H		
I			J			
	K	L			M	
		N			O	P
Q	R			S		
T				U		

Across

A. Q across – N across

D. Consecutive digits in ascending order

G. N across + Q across

H. A palindrome

I. C down × 3

J. J down / C down

K. Contains one of every odd digit

N. O across – R down

O. A perfect square

Q. C down squared

S. Q across × 2

T. D across × 3

U. E down × I across

Down

A. A across + 2

B. Another palindrome

C. N across + 1

D. T across × 3

E. Sum of the digits in K across

F. E down + 6

J. I across × N across

L. Another palindrome

M. Consecutive digits not in order

P. E down squared

Q. F down in reverse

R. Q down × 2

S. H across – D across

Rows Garden 4

Using the clues provided, enter a letter into each triangle to fill the garden. Each row contains one or two entries, and each hexagonal flower contains a six-letter word wrapped around the center. It's up to you to determine where to place the starting letter and the direction of the word.

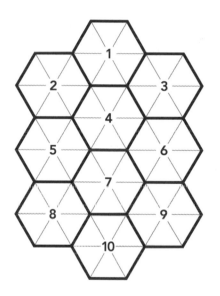

Anxious affliction

Seaweed / Equals

Model Crawford / Informal display

Location of first pride

Facebook parent company / Explorer Polo

Move effortlessly / Area

What seven consumed / Feudal landowners

Farm bug?

Flowers

1.	Obtained to	6.	Formal shirt part
2.	Five cent coin	7.	Awestruck
3.	Tenure as leader	8.	Innermost surface
4.	"Baconator" home	9.	Flying bots
5.	Stacked idols	10.	Shack

Scenic Route 3

Use the clues to determine pairs of words that fit the blanks provided. Each pair will feature one shorter word with only some of the letters, and one longer word that features all of the letters. When complete, the numbered blanks will spell the name of a travel destination.

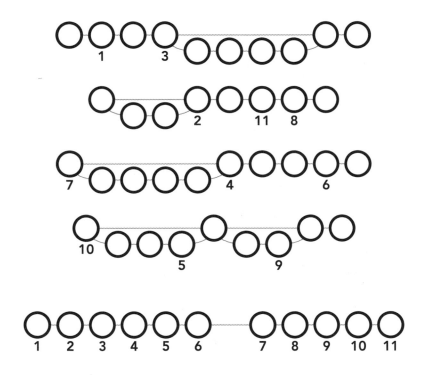

Faster Routes

Adorable

Connecting rope

Fairly

Seething

Scenic Routes

Answer a math problem

Co-located

Someday

Teen's job

Symbol Sums 3

The sums of five combinations of symbols have been provided. What is the value of each individual symbol?

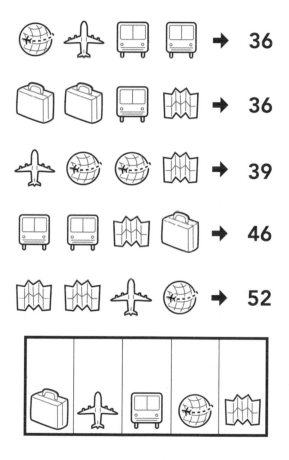

Word Sudoku 3

Place one of each letter from the word below into each row, column, and 2 × 3 box. (Ignore repeated letters.) A bracket between two squares points in the direction of the square with the letter that comes first in the alphabet.

ST. LOUIS

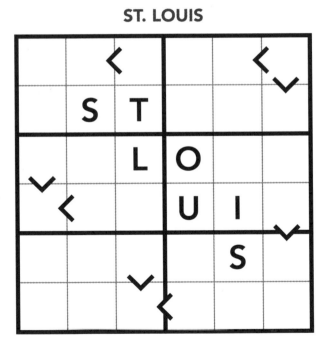

Transit Map 5

Use the clues to fill the bus route with letters to form words both
northbound and southbound.

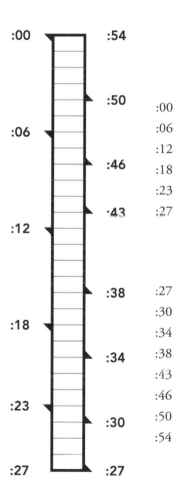

Southbound

:00
:06
:12
:18
:23
:27

Minder
Sitting unused
Neighbor of Sweden
Friend in Mexico
Toss like a millennial

Northbound

:27
:30
:34
:38
:43
:46
:50
:54

Golfer's utility
Noted cartoon bear
Writer Angelou
Incorrect
Nada
Life or death
Sneak a look

Rebus Travel Agency 6

This travel agency has some unusual ways of advertising travel destinations. Can you figure out where they want to send travelers?

TEAUSTXAS

Throwing Shade 5

Shade some cells so the remaining letters in each row and column spell answers to the provided clues. Clues are sorted alphabetically by answer.

B	U	S	I	T	F	T	E	C
R	R	F	O	H	H	O	L	L
M	E	T	R	E	O	R	E	O
O	B	R	I	A	E	I	O	C
C	B	E	N	D	L	S	T	O
C	S	A	N	Y	Y	O	N	E
H	U	M	V	I	T	N	D	A
A	V	Y	E	V	E	O	O	N
A	S	S	R	A	L	N	N	E

Rows

- Skincare brand
- Turns or angles
- Rocky destination
- Hot, wet weather
- Transit org.
- Popular sandwich
- Bread format
- Mentally stable
- Pour through

Columns

- Femme attitude
- Tina of SNL fame
- Place to stay
- Big UK city
- Solo
- Chocolate beverage
- Visual riddle type
- Waterway
- Body section

Symbol Sums 4

The sums of five combinations of symbols have been provided. What is the value of each individual symbol?

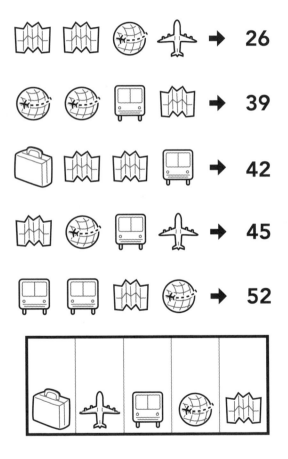

Rearrangement 7 and 8

Rearrange the letters in "SUSHI PRICE" to spell a place where sushi might cost an arm and a leg despite proximity to the ocean.

Rearrange the letters in "BRANDED OCARINA" to spell a location where you might find some gimmicky novelties on the way home from another country.

Lost Luggage 3

What a bummer! Each of the words below has lost the letters from the word LUGGAGE. Use the clues to determine which letters are missing and reunite them to complete the words.

_ _ _ _ _ _   A flock of geese

_ _ _ _   Hawaiian party

_ _ _ _ _   Aquatic blooming lifeform

_ _ _ _ _   Patriotic American bird

_ _ _ _ _ _   Organized group or association

Cube Logic 5

Which of the four foldable patterns can be folded to make the crate displayed?

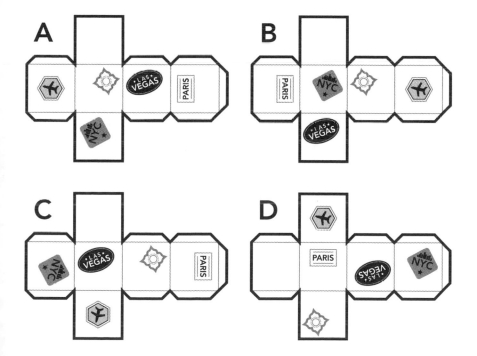

Symbol Sums 5

The sums of five combinations of symbols have been provided. What is the value of each individual symbol?

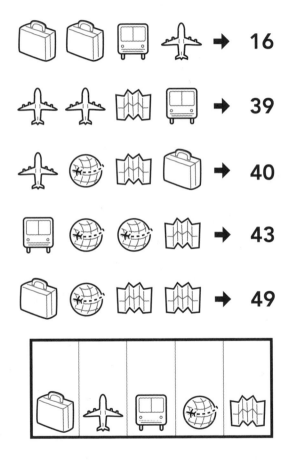

Rebus Travel Agency 7

This travel agency has some unusual ways of advertising travel destinations. Can you figure out where they want to send travelers?

Rows Garden 5

Using the clues provided, enter a letter into each triangle to fill the garden. Each row contains one or two entries, and each hexagonal flower contains a six-letter word wrapped around the center. It's up to you to determine where to place the starting letter and the direction of the word.

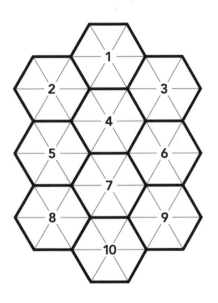

Mr. Brooks or Ms. Giedroyc

Bird-adjacent / Camper's shelter

Witch trial town / Unit of land

Idaho's capital / One of the five tastes

Especially pleased

Subgroup / Common metal

Quick bite / Move gently

A museum topic

Flowers

1. A layer of the earth
2. Mouth contents
3. Align in the middle
4. Popular street or flavor
5. Heated until bubbling
6. Alternate route
7. Dancer's garb
8. Small aircraft brand
9. Some slack
10. Foot or paw prints

Transit Map 6

Use the clues to fill the bus route with letters to form words both northbound and southbound.

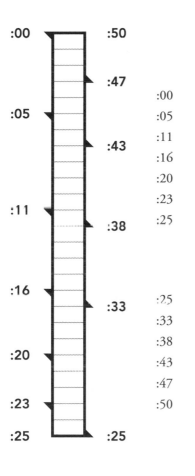

:00		:50
		:47
		:00
:05		:05
		:11
		:43
		:16
		:20
		:23
:11		:25
		:38
:16		
		:25
		:33
		:33
		:38
:20		:43
		:47
:23		:50
:25		:25

Southbound

:00   Little bugs
:05   Bear-adjacent
:11   Satan
:16   Was indebted to
:20   Japanese currency
:23   Deflated utterance

Northbound

:25   Melon variety
:33   Oil type
:38   Comedian Leary
:43   Facade
:47   Actor Curry

Throwing Shade 6

Shade some cells so the remaining letters in each row and column spell answers to the provided clues. Clues are sorted alphabetically by answer.

H	A	R	L	E	O	C	N	E
E	T	L	A	C	T	H	C	H
E	T	I	S	O	L	A	N	D
M	O	V	S	T	I	A	E	E
C	H	A	C	H	A	I	R	R
P	L	V	U	T	G	N	S	O
S	L	E	E	I	I	D	E	O
V	I	R	B	O	G	L	T	O
P	L	R	A	N	M	E	O	P

Rows

- Door mechanism
- Furniture item
- Carve lightly
- Tortoise rival
- Landmass
- August birth
- Film
- Arithmetic symbol
- Sloped surface

Columns

- Landmasses
- Allow to fall
- Follower of Delta
- Frozen precipitation
- Plant used in textiles
- Actor Hemsworth
- Bird dwelling
- Waterway
- Diving apparatus

Rebus Travel Agency 8

This travel agency has some unusual ways of advertising travel destinations. Can you figure out where they want to send travelers?

LAFND

Numcross 6

Use the provided clues to fill the grid with numbers. No entry may start with a 0.

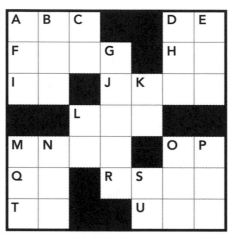

Across

A. A palindrome

D. Square root of P down

F. N down × 6

H. D across + I across

I. Square root of A down

J. Digits that sum to a perfect square

L. Consecutive digits not in order

M. One-half of F across

O. I across + 1

Q. T across + 4

R. Digits that sum to K down

T. S down – I across

U. P down + 200

Down

A. I across squared

B. D down × 3

C. O across + 1

D. Contains the digits from D across and K down

E. Consecutive digits in ascending order

G. Consecutive digits not in order

K. A perfect cube

L. K down × 3

M. O across squared

N. I across × T across

O. A multiple of I across

P. One-third of L across

S. K down × 2

Rearrangement 9 and 10

Rearrange the letters in "VIP GALA STRESS" to make a location in the desert where some gaudy partying might take place.

Rearrange the letters in "SOCIAL NUCLEI" to spell a good reason to go out and meet people in a new place.

Rebus Travel Agency 9

This travel agency has some unusual ways of advertising travel destinations. Can you figure out where they want to send travelers?

Country Road 3

Draw a single, continuous, non-intersecting loop moving through the grid and visiting each boldly outlined region exactly once. A region displaying a number indicates the number of cells visited in that region. Non-visited cells from two different regions mustn't share an edge.

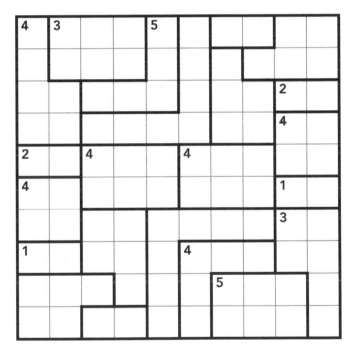

Cube Logic 6

Which of the four foldable patterns can be folded to make the crate displayed?

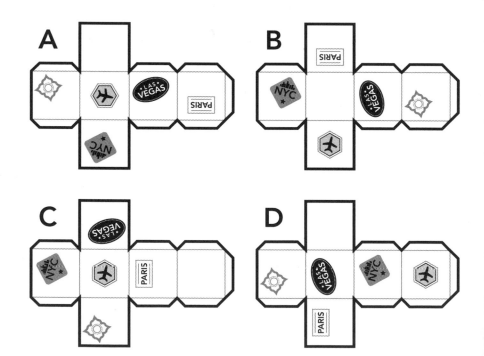

Rearrangement 11 and 12

Rearrange the letters in "DORK PARADISE" to spell a location where nerdy types might stop to read a historic marker.

Rearrange the letters in "WET HITTING WARFARE" to spell an adventure you could call the ultimate battle pitting man and boat versus rocks and rivers.

Numcross 7

Use the provided clues to fill the grid with numbers. No entry may start with a 0.

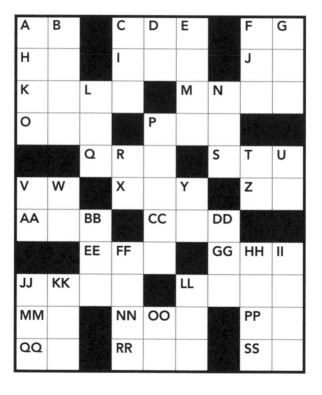

Across

A. F across in reverse

C. V across × 2

F. MM across − 1

H. One-fourth of J across

I. C down × 4

J. F across × 5

K. An anagram of A down

M. E down in reverse

O. MM across × PP across

P. N down in reverse

Q. Z across × PP across

S. GG across − 4

V. J across + 1

X. T down × Y down

Z. GG across / Y down

AA. F across + O across

CC. DD down in reverse

EE. AA across + GG across

GG. A palindrome

JJ. Another palindrome

LL. MM across × G down

MM. T down in reverse

NN. C across in reverse

PP. One-half of J across

QQ. J across + Y down

RR. Consecutive digits in some order

SS. U down in reverse

Down

A. An anagram of HH across

B. One-fourth of JJ across

C. F down + 1

D. A perfect square

E. M across in reverse

F. U down × 2

G. S across − R down

L. KK down − OO down

N. T down + U down

P. Contains one of every even digit

R. Another perfect square

T. R down − 5

U. Another perfect square

V. Another perfect square

W. One-third of PP across

Y. Z across × 2

BB. OO down × 9

DD. One-eighth of II down

FF. All but one of the digits in P down, in some order

HH. Consecutive digits not in order

II. One-eighth of P down

JJ. L down × 6

KK. F across × Z across

LL. NN across − 4

OO. R down − 7

Rebus Travel Agency 10

This travel agency has some unusual ways of advertising travel destinations. Can you figure out where they want to send travelers?

Rearrangement 13, 14, 15

Rearrange the letters in "TOSSED FOREWORD" to spell a location where tall and mighty trees might leave a writer speechless.

Rearrange the letters in "FLUTTERY BOATIES" to spell a monument that requires zipping across the water on a ferry to visit.

Rearrange the letters in "A RODENT ALMANAC" to spell a French-speaking city where you might see a mouse or two.

Rows Garden 6

Using the clues provided, enter a letter into each triangle to fill the garden. Each row contains one or two entries, and each hexagonal flower contains a six-letter word wrapped around the center. It's up to you to determine where to place the starting letter and the direction of the word.

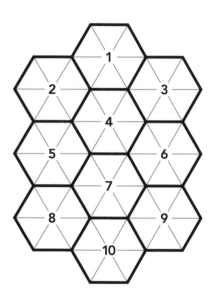

Actor Liotta

Defeats / Junk

A gulf coast state

Evil entity / Guilty pleasure

Type of pet or seed / Record

Old radio controls / Top of a house

Divide / Snow vessel

Dude

Flowers

1. Alley cats

2. Garment

3. Home of a famed canal

4. Sight

5. Rang

6. Politely

7. Bitter foes

8. Tartans

9. Tricked

10. Paths around something

Symbol Sums 6

The sums of five combinations of symbols have been provided. What is the value of each individual symbol?

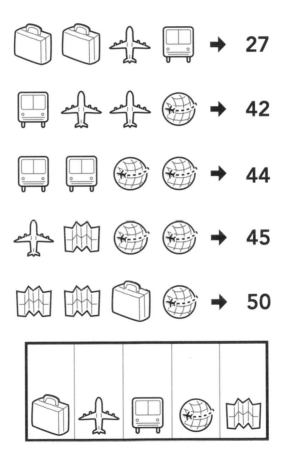

Cube Logic 7

Which of the four foldable patterns can be folded to make the crate displayed?

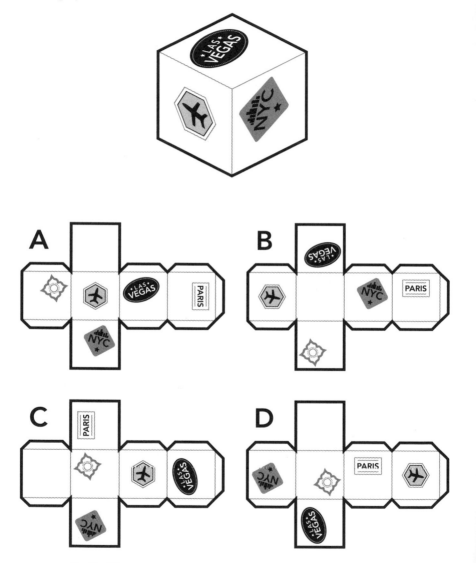

Lost Luggage 4

Oof! Worse than Lost Luggage 1-3, each of the words below *and its clue* have lost the letters from the word LUGGAGE. Determine which letters are missing and reunite them to complete the clues and words.

_R_ _M_NT   V_rb_ _ fi_ht

S_ND_ _S   Op_n-to_d sho_s

S_ _V_ _ _   R_c_ _im wh_t's _ _ft

S_ _ _PY   N_ _din_ _ n_p

CO_ _ _ _ _   Hi_h_r _d_c_tion

Scenic Route 4

Use the clues to determine pairs of words that fit the blanks provided. Each pair will feature one shorter word with only some of the letters, and one longer word that features all of the letters. When complete, the numbered blanks will spell the name of a travel destination.

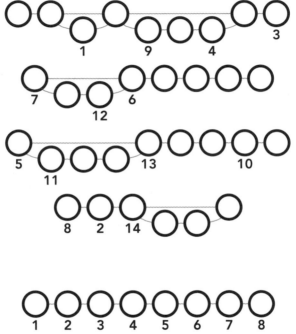

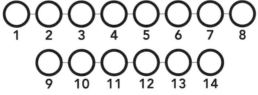

Faster Routes

Originating within

Over

Romantic partners

To a great degree

Scenic Routes

Backer

Contribute

Less than zero

Yesterday's dinner

Rebus Travel Agency 11

This travel agency has some unusual ways of advertising travel destinations. Can you figure out where they want to send travelers?

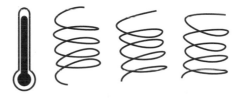

Throwing Shade 7

Shade some cells so the remaining letters in each row and column spell answers to the provided clues. Clues are sorted alphabetically by answer.

B	O	S	T	A	T	A	Y	S
S	R	O	F	F	A	T	F	A
H	C	C	O	O	S	N	E	H
A	A	R	C	C	A	A	R	C
W	O	R	I	N	B	B	S	D
W	N	O	R	R	W	T	L	H
S	G	B	O	W	L	L	O	E
V	P	O	L	T	S	E	R	A
E	E	W	A	T	E	R	T	R

Rows

- Curve
- Ice cream holder
- Spheres
- Court utterance
- Living room item
- Lone
- Hotel visits
- One of the elements
- Value

Columns

- Poker buy-in
- Soda flavor
- Officer
- Military place
- Woodworker tools
- Cut or trim
- Somber mood
- Dining room item
- Affirmative

Word Sudoku 4

Place one of each letter from the word below into each row, column, and 2 × 3 box. A bracket between two squares points in the direction of the square with the letter that comes first in the alphabet.

ST. PAUL

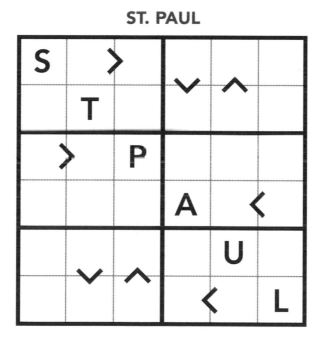

Transit Map 7

Use the clues to fill the bus route with letters to form words both
northbound and southbound.

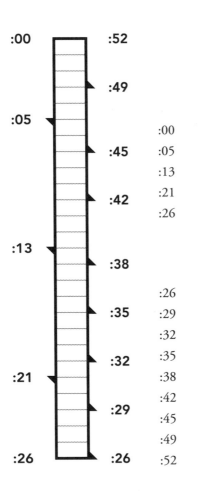

:00	:52
:05	:49
	:45
	:42
:13	:38
	:35
	:32
:21	:29
:26	:26

Southbound

:00
:05
:13
:21
:26

Toothy reptile
Event guest
Preparing gifts
Like some bygone days

Northbound

:26
:29
:32
:35
:38
:42
:45
:49
:52

Mr. Flanders
Cabin-building material
Bite at
Golfer's goal
Garden invader
Fishing tool
Purple root veg
Clothing label

Rows Garden 7

Using the clues provided, enter a letter into each triangle to fill the garden. Each row contains one or two entries, and each hexagonal flower contains a six-letter word wrapped around the center. It's up to you to determine where to place the starting letter and the direction of the word.

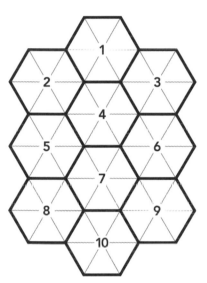

Seasonal Starbucks offering, briefly

Transaction / Slim gradually

Doctor Who baddie / Greenish blue

Immersive puzzle hunts / Focused energy beam

Highway travel center

Bar furniture / Sporting good

Unit of land / Senator Rubio

Two-patty burger, briefly

Flowers

1.	Flower parts	6.	Magic word
2.	Big Texan City	7.	Toys for building
3.	Overturn	8.	Type of oil
4.	Potato pancakes	9.	Shirt feature
5.	Toddler	10.	Held responsible

Throwing Shade 8

Shade some cells so the remaining letters in each row and column spell answers to the provided clues. Clues are sorted alphabetically by answer.

E	C	L	L	B	E	O	W	W
E	C	A	A	B	S	W	H	O
A	S	Q	A	U	A	C	A	H
S	A	U	C	G	A	E	R	A
C	M	A	S	H	S	U	F	O
Q	A	U	C	I	I	I	Y	D
U	M	E	D	U	N	R	A	D
T	O	R	C	G	N	D	T	R
S	Y	Y	E	R	T	I	U	P

Rows

- Opposite of base
- Turquoise
- Bills
- Body part
- Pill, for example
- Sweetener
- Ripped
- Spacecraft, maybe
- Cryptid

Columns

- Issue
- Army pattern
- Sunrise direction
- Frilly cloth
- Unusual
- French agreement
- Question
- Holy figure
- Coastal structure

Cube Logic 8

Which of the four foldable patterns can be folded to make the crate displayed?

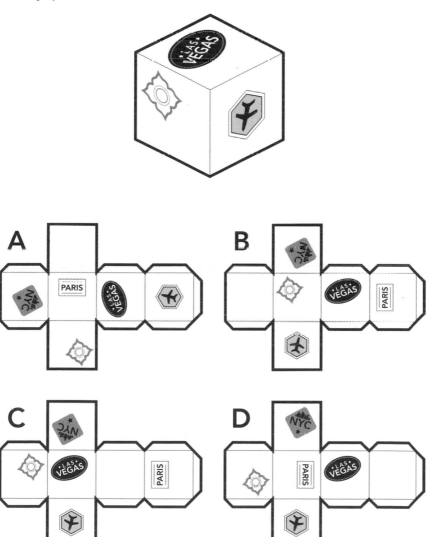

Word Sudoku 5

Place one of each letter from the word below into each row, column, and 3 × 3 box. (Ignore repeated letters.) A bracket between two squares points in the direction of the square with the letter that comes first in the alphabet.

PUGET SOUND

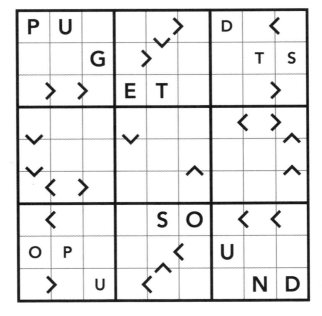

Country Road 4

Draw a single, continuous, non-intersecting loop moving through the grid and visiting each boldly outlined region exactly once. A region displaying a number indicates the number of cells visited in that region. Non-visited cells from two different regions mustn't share an edge.

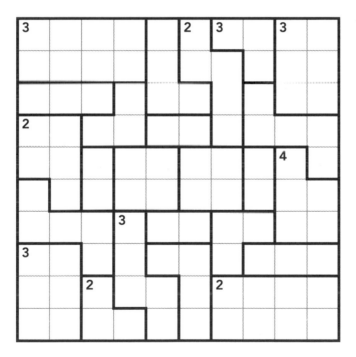

Rows Garden 8

Using the clues provided, enter a letter into each triangle to fill the garden. Each row contains one or two entries, and each hexagonal flower contains a six-letter word wrapped around the center. It's up to you to determine where to place the starting letter and the direction of the word.

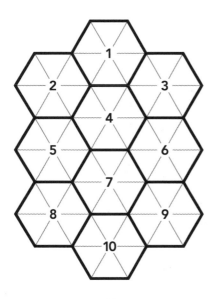

Purple veg

Adjust spacing / Toothy mechanisms

Light attribute / Libs

California and friends

Shout / Data storage device

The Simpsons daughter / Traveler

Morning, e.g. / Fury

Period

Flowers

1. Type of cord
2. Storage place in gyms
3. Streaky applications
4. Health professional
5. Actor Snipes

6. Low-cal sweetener
7. Burger clown
8. Middle East country
9. Break
10. Infrequently

Transit Map 8

Use the clues to fill the bus route with letters to form words both northbound and southbound.

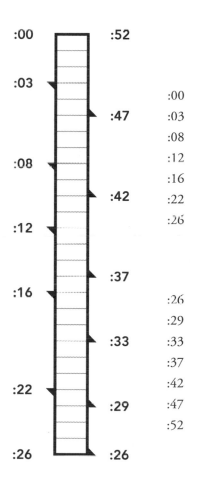

Southbound

:00
:03
:08
:12
:16
:22
:26

Light meaning stop
Citrus fruit
Equal
Middle of the foot
Finn's friend
Unbridled joy

Northbound

:26
:29
:33
:37
:42
:47
:52

Slippery sea creature
Dr. Meredith
Clean up
Large bird
Snake or spider spit
Person of age

Throwing Shade 9

Shade some cells so the remaining letters in each row and column spell answers to the provided clues. Clues are sorted alphabetically by answer.

C	W	H	I	R	I	E	R	E
R	D	O	D	I	G	I	T	T
C	I	T	Y	T	T	I	Y	R
T	O	D	L	B	A	W	N	G
A	S	O	I	S	I	I	P	O
R	R	U	L	Y	U	S	L	E
A	B	N	E	P	A	G	E	L
M	M	A	S	S	I	H	E	U
T	H	G	E	E	A	T	R	T

Rows

- Tree topper
- Carrier
- Metropolis
- Finger, for example
- Warmth
- Break up
- Law
- Drink slowly
- Cord

Columns

- Force in
- Common figure
- Mother Earth
- Ooze
- Motionless
- BBQ staple
- Common fish
- Variety
- Cheap online shop

Word Sudoku 6

Place one of each letter from the word below into each row, column, and 3 × 3 box. (Ignore repeated letters.) A bracket between two squares points in the direction of the square with the letter that comes first in the alphabet.

MACKINAC ISLAND

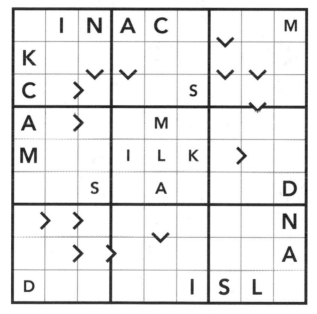

Numcross 8

Use the provided clues to fill the grid with numbers. No entry may start with a 0.

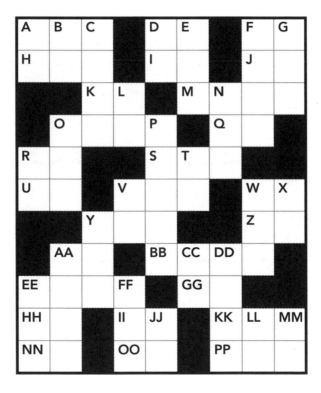

Across

A. A down × GG across

D. D down – 1

F. L down – MM down

H. A multiple of R across

I. Sum of the digits in O across

J. A multiple of R across

K. I across – 4

M. Contains the digits that are not in O across or Q across

O. Contains the digits that are not in M across or Q across

Q. A perfect square

R. Number of ones needed in the bottom half of the grid, including the middle row

S. E down × 7

U. W across + 1

V. NN across + PP across

W. X down – 2

Y. N down × 3

Z. T down × 2

AA. Another perfect square

BB. 3 × Y across

EE. O across × 3

GG. A prime number

HH. D across + W across

II. LL down – 3

KK. OO across × 3

NN. JJ down + 1

OO. If LL down is even, this is LL down – 10, otherwise it's 2 × LL down

PP. Another perfect square

Down

A. D across × 2

B. F down / AA across

C. Year Olympians went to PyeongChang for the winter games

D. A multiple of R down

E. N down – 8

F. B down × AA across

G. II across + PP across

L. A multiple of R down

N. A palindrome

O. M across / NN across

P. Contains one of each odd digit

R. Another perfect square

T. Q across – 10

V. A factor of MM down

W. HH across × 7

X. Contains even digits that are not in MM down

Y. A multiple of G down

AA. Consecutive digits not in order

CC. JJ down × 1.5

DD. W down × 9

EE. AA across × GG across

FF. GG across × NN across

JJ. GG across + 3

LL. A perfect cube

MM. One-sixth of PP across

Rows Garden 9

Using the clues provided, enter a letter into each triangle to fill the garden. Each row contains one or two entries, and each hexagonal flower contains a six-letter word wrapped around the center. It's up to you to determine where to place the starting letter and the direction of the word.

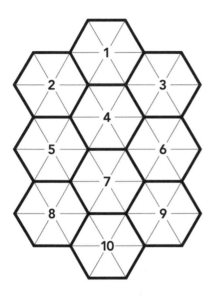

Result of addition

Body region / Bit of land

Location of some pirates

Bring up / Yogurt sauce

Some birds / Break swiftly

Parrot / Express yourself

Telegraph code / Fraud

Mario machine, once

Flowers

1. Nocturnal animal
2. Frosty nose
3. Shanty
4. Tortoise foe
5. Chemex component

6. External appearance
7. Soup mates
8. Like Safari
9. Theater
10. Finds

Cube Logic 9

Which of the four foldable patterns can be folded to make the crate displayed?

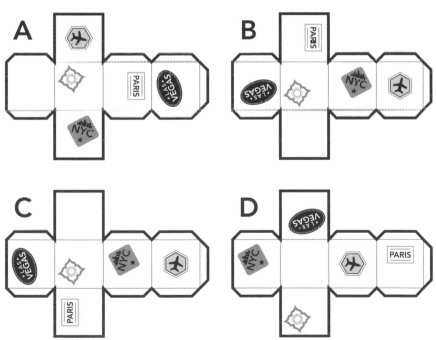

Lost Luggage 5

Oof! Worse than Lost Luggage 1-3, each of the words below *and its clue* have lost the letters from the word LUGGAGE. Determine which letters are missing and reunite them to complete the clues and words.

_ _ _OON   _qu_tic _oc_tion

_ _I_N   _xtr_t_rr_stri_ _

M_N_ _ _   _ _id_ book_ _t

_ _R_IC   _rom_tic v_mpir_ r_p_ _ _ _nt

_ _ _ _ON   Mi_k j_ _ siz_

Scenic Route 5

Use the clues to determine pairs of words that fit the blanks provided. Each pair will feature one shorter word with only some of the letters, and one longer word that features all of the letters. When complete, the numbered blanks will spell the name of a travel destination.

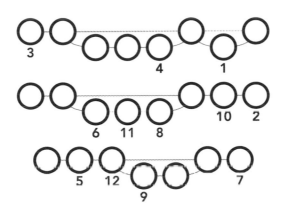

Faster Routes

Be patient
Group of trees
Shred

Scenic Routes

Break apart
Rock sometimes used in countertops
Spot on a route

Cube Logic 10

Which of the four foldable patterns can be folded to make the crate displayed?

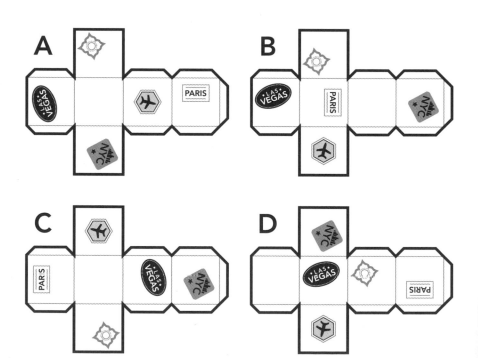

Transit Map 9

Use the clues to fill the bus route with letters to form words both northbound and southbound.

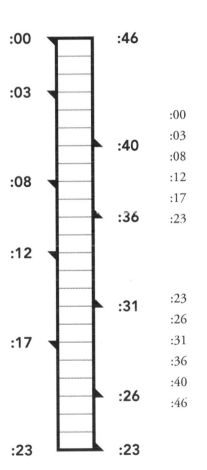

:00   :46

:03

:40

:08

:36

:12

:31

:17

:26

:23   :23

Southbound

:00
:03   Droplets on grass
:08   Tree-topper
:12   T-rex, for one
:17   Satellite competitor
:23   Hook and loop material

Northbound

:23   Larping baddie
:26   Stage
:31   Breakfast meat
:36   Stationary
:40   Chewed
:46

Lost Luggage 6

Oof! Worse than Lost Luggage 1-3, each of the words below *and its clue* have lost the letters from the word LUGGAGE. Determine which letters are missing and reunite them to complete the clues and words.

_ _ _ _   _r_ _t wind forc_

_ _ _ _ _   _ _ _ow_d by _ _w

_ _ _   Si_ _y pr_nk

_ _ _ _ _   _ _ _ from F_t_r_m_

_ _ _ _   Sin_ _r Fitz_ _r_ _d

Rows Garden 10

Using the clues provided, enter a letter into each triangle to fill the garden. Each row contains one or two entries, and each hexagonal flower contains a six-letter word wrapped around the center. It's up to you to determine where to place the starting letter and the direction of the word.

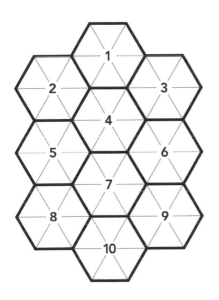

Soviet space station

Bits of paper / Flavorful plant

Former student / To a great degree

Empty / Narrow opening

Plans for a car?

Tall plant / Every 24 hours

Celebrity / Lid

Everything

Flowers

1.   Little seafood

2.   Coveted items

3.   Haggle

4.   Muddy goop

5.   A fuss

6.   Frequent fliers

7.   Swapped

8.   Goodies

9.   Outer branding

10.   Pet wearable

Answer Keys

Country Road

Country Road 1

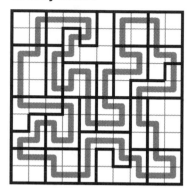

Country Road 2

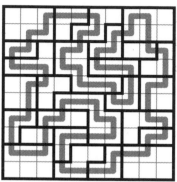

Country Road 3

Country Road 4

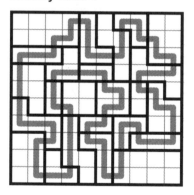

Cube Logic

1. A and E
2. C and D
3. B and D
4. B

5. D
6. A
7. A
8. C

9. D
10. B

Lost Luggage

Lost Luggage 1
  Vulgar
  Lounge
  Castle
  Leggings
  Gelatin

Lost Luggage 2
  Sugar
  Dragon
  Gluten
  Angel
  Agent

Lost Luggage 3
  Gaggle
  Luau
  Algae
  Eagle
  League

Lost Luggage 4
  Argument (Verbal fight)
  Sandals (Open-toed shoes)
  Salvage (Reclaim what's left)
  Sleepy (Needing a nap)
  College (Higher education)

Lost Luggage 5
  Lagoon (Aquatic location)
  Alien (Extraterrestrial)
  Manual (Guide booklet)
  Garlic (Aromatic vampire repellant)
  Gallon (Milk jug size)

Lost Luggage 6
  Gale (Great wind force)
  Legal (Allowed by law)
  Gag (Silly prank)
  Leela (Gal from Futurama)
  Ella (Singer Fitzgerald)

Numcross

Numcross 1

1	2	3			4	5
7	1	4	1		3	5
1	0		3	5	2	9
		4	9	5		
1	4	1	7		3	6
2	5		5	5	9	0
1	1				3	6	0

Numcross 2

7	2	7			7	7
2	1	2	1		7	0
3	0		4	3	7	7
		7	7	6		
7	7	3	4		2	7
1	3		2	1	0	0
1	0			6	7	0

Numcross 3

3	8	3			8	6
1	9	9	1		9	2
9	1		5	7	7	5
		6	3	8		
1	9	8	1		1	3
1	0		2	5	5	2
8	7			2	6	1

Numcross 4

2	5	3		1	3	2
2	4	8		1	1	3
5	3		1	1		
	2	9	5	1	5	
	1	9		9	5	
5	2	5		4	0	7
5	5	0		4	3	0

Numcross 5

1	1	1		1	2	3
1	3	1		1	5	1
3	3		3	0		
	1	9	3	7	5	
	1	0		3	6	
1	2	1		2	4	2
3	6	9		8	2	5

Numcross 6

1	3	1			1	7
2	8	3	8		2	8
1	1		7	2	7	9
		8	6	7		
1	4	1	9		1	2
4	7		5	5	9	8
4	3			4	8	9

Numcross 7

2	1		1	2	2		1	2
1	5		6	5	2		6	0
4	2	1	3		1	1	2	2
3	9	0		2	1	1		
		3	3	0		2	3	8
6	1		6	8	2		1	1
4	0	2		6	2	3		
		6	4	4		2	4	2
6	1	1	6		2	6	2	6
1	3		2	2	1		3	0
8	2		8	9	7		1	8

Numcross 8

6	8	2		3	1		7	2
2	9	0		2	3		2	0
		1	9		3	1	0	5
	2	8	6	7		4	9	
1	0		9	3	1			
6	7		1	5	9		6	6
	4	2	3				7	8
	8	1		1	2	6	9	
8	6	0	1		1	1		
9	7		6	1		1	6	2
1	5		5	4		1	4	4

Rearrangement

1. Grand Canyon
2. Peppered Turkey Jerky
3. Florence, Italy
4. Terminal Shuttle
5. Miniature Golf
6. Backpacking Trip
7. Cruise Ship
8. Canadian Border
9. Las Vegas Strip
10. Local Cuisine
11. Roadside Park
12. Whitewater Rafting
13. Redwood Forests
14. Statue of Liberty
15. Montreal, Canada

Rebus Travel Agency

1. Little Rock
2. Scenic Overlook
3. Arizona
4. London, UK
5. Long Beach
6. Austin, Texas
7. Portland, Maine
8. Finland
9. Loch Ness
10. Santa Fe
11. Hot Springs

Rows Garden

Rows Garden 1

```
      E D M
D E R P P A D R E
T O U M S L E E P
K E T O D E C O R
C U B A S O L A R
U M A M I M E S A
S E D A N A C R E
      N A B
```

Rows Garden 2

```
      T I N
T E N E I G H T Y
O D O R I C I N G
R O U T E M O L E
A F T E R M A T H
I N E P T I D L E
C A M E O M O O N
      S K I
```

Rows Garden 3

```
      T O M
T I M E R E L M O
C O M E T T A T S
L I A R B E L L E
D E T E N T I O N
S W I R L A R I D
L E V E E M E L D
      R I P
```

Rows Garden 4

```
      O C D
K E L P P E E R S
C I N D Y S I G N
S T O N E W A L L
M E T A M A R C O
G L I D E Z O N E
N I N E L O R D S
      A N T
```

Rows Garden 5

```
      M E L
A V I A N T E N T
S A L E M A C R E
B O I S E S O U R
D E L I G H T E D
S E C T S T E E L
S N A C K S W A Y
      A R T
```

Rows Garden 6

```
      R A Y
B E S T S S P A M
L O U I S I A N A
D E M O N V I C E
C H I A V I N Y L
D I A L S R O O F
S P L I T S L E D
      B R O
```

Rows Garden 7

```
      P S L
S A L E T A P E R
D A L E K T E A L
A R G S L A S E R
T R U C K S T O P
S T O O L B A L L
A C R E M A R C O
      D B L
```

Rows Garden 8

```
      U B E
K E R N G E A R S
C O L O R D E M S
W E S T C O A S T
Y E L L D R I V E
L I S A N O M A D
E A R L Y R A G E
      E R A
```

Scenic Route

Scenic Route 1

Convent / Convenient

Uncle / Uncomfortable

Dimed / Disarmed

Lining / Listening

Galveston Island

Scenic Route 2

Diver / Deliver

Poster / Polyester

Board / Bombard

Biding / Building

Empire Builder

Scenic Route 3

Evenly / Eventually

Tether / Together

Bitter / Babysitter

Cute / Calculate

Venice Beach

Scenic Route 4

Super / Supporter

Native / Negative

Lovers / Leftovers

Done / Donate

Portland, Oregon

Scenic Route 5

Wait / Waypoint

Copse / Collapse

Grate / Granite

New Orleans, LA

Story Logic

Story Logic 1

- First was the roseate spoonbill photo taken by Evan. Second was the American redstart photo taken by Colby. Third was the black skimmer photo taken by Eli. Fourth was the scarlet tanager photo taken by Alan. Fifth was the cerulean warbler photo taken by Mark.

Story Logic 2

- In early June, Dinesh is booked for Las Vegas. In late June, Dawn is booked for Los Angeles. In early July, Miguel is booked for NYC. In late July, Carly is booked for Seattle. In early August, Marco is booked for Hawaii.

Symbol Sums

Symbol Sums 1

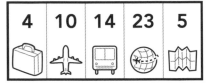

Symbol Sums 2

Symbol Sums 3

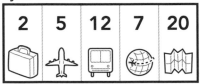

Symbol Sums 4

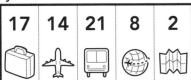

Symbol Sums 5

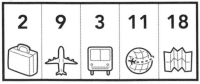

Symbol Sums 6

Throwing Shade

Throwing Shade 1

Throwing Shade 2

Throwing Shade 3

Throwing Shade 4

Throwing Shade 5

Throwing Shade 6

Throwing Shade 7

Throwing Shade 8

Throwing Shade 9

Transit Map 1

Southbound

:00	
	Spill
:05	
	Aides
:10	
	Organs
:16	
	Sample
:22	
	Hoot
:26	

Northbound

:26	
	Too
:29	
	Help
:33	
	Mass
:37	
	Nag
:40	
	Rose
:44	
	Dial
:48	
	Lips
:52	

Transit Map 2

Southbound

:00	
	Bar
:03	
	Citizen
:10	
	Order
:15	
	Affixed
:22	
	Alas
:26	

Northbound

:26	
	Salad
:31	
	EXIF
:35	
	Fare
:39	
	Drone
:44	
	Ziti
:48	
	Crab
:52	

Transit Map 3

Southbound

:00	
	Flu
:03	
	Glow
:07	
	Amish
:12	
	Cradle
:18	
	HD
:20	
	Nah
:23	

Northbound

:23	
	Handheld
:31	
	Arch
:35	
	Sim
:38	
	AWOL
:42	
	Gulf
:46	

Transit Map 4

Southbound

:00	
	Liar
:04	
	Texas
:09	
	Sarge
:14	
	Garden
:20	
	Nuts
:24	

Northbound

:24	
	Stunned
:31	
	Rage
:35	
	Grass
:40	
	Axe
:43	
	Trail
:48	

Transit Map 5

Southbound

:00
:06   Keeper
:12   Idling
:18   Norway
:23   Amigo
:27   Yeet

Northbound

:27
:30   Tee
:34   Yogi
:38   Maya
:43   Wrong
:46   Nil
:50   Dire
:54   Peek

Transit Map 6

Southbound

:00
:05   Mites
:11   Ursine
:16   Devil
:20   Owed
:23   Yen
:25   Oh

Northbound

:25
:33   Honeydew
:38   Olive
:43   Denis
:47   Ruse
:50   Tim

Transit Map 7

Southbound

:00
:05   Gator
:13   Attendee
:21   Wrapping
:26   Olden

Northbound

:26
:29   Ned
:32   Log
:35   Nip
:38   Par
:42   Weed
:45   Net
:49   Taro
:52   Tag

Transit Map 8

Southbound

:00
:03   Red
:08   Lemon
:12   Even
:16   Arch
:22   Sawyer
:26   Glee

Northbound

:26
:29   Eel
:33   Grey
:37   Wash
:42   Crane
:47   Venom
:52   Elder

Transit Map 9

Southbound

:00	
:03	Dew
:08	Angel
:12	Dino
:17	Cable
:23	Velcro

Northbound

:23	
:26	Orc
:31	Level
:36	Bacon
:40	Idle
:46	Gnawed

Word Sudoku

Word Sudoku 1

O	N	A	R	I	Z
R	Z	I	N	A	O
A	R	Z	I	O	N
N	I	O	Z	R	A
I	A	N	O	Z	R
Z	O	R	A	N	I

Word Sudoku 2

M	I	U	R	S	O
R	O	S	I	U	M
I	M	R	S	O	U
U	S	O	M	I	R
O	R	I	U	M	S
S	U	M	O	R	I

Word Sudoku 3

I	O	U	S	L	T
L	S	T	I	U	O
U	I	L	O	T	S
O	T	S	U	I	L
T	U	O	L	S	I
S	L	I	T	O	U

Word Sudoku 4

S	U	L	T	A	P
P	T	A	L	S	U
T	A	P	U	L	S
U	L	S	A	P	T
L	S	T	P	U	A
A	P	U	S	T	L

Word Sudoku 5

P	U	T	S	O	G	D	E	N
E	O	G	N	D	U	P	T	S
S	N	D	E	T	P	G	U	O
U	D	P	T	G	S	N	O	E
N	E	S	O	U	D	T	G	P
G	T	O	P	E	N	S	D	U
D	G	N	U	S	O	E	P	T
O	P	E	D	N	T	U	S	G
T	S	U	G	P	E	O	N	D

Word Sudoku 6

S	I	N	A	C	L	K	D	M
K	A	L	N	D	M	I	S	C
C	M	D	K	I	S	A	N	L
A	N	K	S	M	D	L	C	I
M	D	C	I	L	K	N	A	S
I	L	S	C	A	N	M	K	D
L	K	I	D	S	A	C	M	N
N	S	M	L	K	C	D	I	A
D	C	A	M	N	I	S	L	K

Exercise Your Mind at American Mensa®

At American Mensa, we love puzzles. In fact, we have events—large and small—centered around games and puzzles.

Of course, with tens of thousands of members from ages 2 to 102, we are much more than that. Our one shared trait might be one you share, too: high intelligence, measured in the top 2 percent of the general public in a standardized test.

Get-togethers with other Mensans—from small pizza nights up to larger events like our annual Mind Games®—are always stimulating and fun. Roughly 130 Special Interest Groups (we call them SIGs) offer the best of the real and virtual worlds. Highlighting the Mensa newsstand is our award-winning magazine, *Mensa Bulletin*, which stimulates the curious mind with unique features that add perspective to our fast-paced world.

And then there are the practical benefits of membership, such as exclusive offers through our partners and member discounts on magazine subscriptions, online shopping, and financial services.

Find out how to qualify or take our practice test at americanmensa.org/join.